NORTH BEACH POEMS

by

A. D. Winans

SECOND COMING PRESS

ACKNOWLEDGMENTS

Gallimaufry, Hyperion, Beatitude, West Conscious Review, Moondance, Desperado, Vagabond, Three Mountains Press, Coldspring Journal, Nitty Gritty, Second Coming, Cave and Thorp Springs Press.

Photograph of Lawrence Ferlinghetti facing page 1 and photograph of Jack Hirschman and Harold Norse on page 6 are by Samuel A. Cherry, father of poet Neeli Cherkovski.

Photograph of A.D. Winans and Jack Micheline on page 8 is by Joel Deutch, local poet, photographer and freelance writer.

Cover photo of "Hobo" and the rest of the photos in the book are by Richard Morris. While a student at the University of Nevada, Richard Morris made his living as a freelance photographer. His photographs appeared in newspapers and magazines and were carried on the AP wires. In 1974 he took up photography again, after a lapse of some years. Since then, his work has been appearing in little magazines and small press books. He has published six books of poetry and two plays. The most recent are *Poetry is a Kind of Writing* (Thorp Springs Press), *Plays* (Twowindows Press) and *The Board of Directors* (Ghost Dance Press).

Copyright © 1977 by Second Coming Press

Library of Congress Catalog Card No. 77-72703
ISBN: 0-915016-11-7 (paperbound)
ISBN: 0-915016-15-X (clothbound)

SECOND COMING PRESS
P.O. Box 31249
San Francisco, CA 94131

for joanie who was here

for ed lipman who died too soon

for jack micheline who influenced the change in me

for those in prison and those who have been there

and for the few live poets who still walk the streets of north beach free of the politicians who control poetry and the stalkers of death who surround them.

This book was partially supported by a grant from The National Endowment for the Arts, Washington, D.C.

North Beach Poems

A. D. Winans

Lawrence Ferlinghetti in front of City Lights Publishing.

FOR LAWRENCE FERLINGHETTI
AND THE OLD REVOLUTION

why must you wait for the harvest
to fail in russia before you don
your sailor suit again and walk
the rusted decks of a ghost ship
that never knew a siberian snowfield
or saw a frozen wheatfield

why worry if the props won't thresh
or there's blood in your drink
they'll never find you down in
the boiler room stoking the fire

you're the admiral of the beats
yet missed kerouac's wake because
they say you don't like funerals

of course nothing moves
it never does for someone
who has forgotten how to dance
in the streets

Vesuvio's Bar

BETRAYED

I saw you Superman
Exposing yourself in
A Chinatown alley on
A sunny April Fool
Morning.

Dick Tracy didn't think
It was so funny
He had you by the balls
Until you convinced
Him you were working on
The side of the law and
Sent him down to
Vesuvio's to arrest
A madman for masturbating in
The streets.

You should have told him
King Kong was down there
You should have told him
King Kong didn't like cops.

God Damn Man
How can
I ever hope to believe in
You again.

Grant Avenue

GRANT AND GREEN

corner of grant and green
six black cats hung and
well done over eye
the young white chick walking
braless through their ranks
their eyes never leave
her swinging buttocks until
she disappears down
the street

only then do
i pass

the eyes are sullen and
say nothing strange
the rapport should disappear
so rapidly

Jack Hirschman and Harold Norse (Cafe Trieste)

NORTH BEACH HAPPENINGS

these poets won't lay down
and die
they insist on walking
the streets
like something out
of creature features.

gathering at
the triest cafe
or shuffling along
grant avenue on their
way to city lights publishing
where old lawrence
the caretaker of the cemetery
closes the door in their faces.

their screams drifting back
down the street where
the ghost of ferlinghetti's
old dying Italian men scale
invisible walls
like a cat minus nine lives
rubbing himself back
to life again.

A.D. Winans and Jack Micheline outside "Books Plus"

listening to jack micheline
read at the northeast mental center
the smell of strawberries in
the air

the words a soft magic
with a mood all
its own chasing away
the mad dreams
their fears riding free down
the corridor

leaving behind poems on
the branches
of dead
trees

words swallowed
like a fire-eaters supper
hearts of madness
hearts of despair
eyes of children cutting through
the headstones
of death

the words balanced by
the jazz man's horn
falling gently as feathers
from a plumed
ostrich.

A.D. Winans and Paddy O'Sullivan (Cafe Trieste)

FOR PADDY O'SULLIVAN

Paddy O' Sullivan
home again wearing
the scars of the past
like an engraved bracelet
passed on from one lover to another
walking the streets of north beach
in search of old visions now only
memories in the nightmare mirror
of madness — swapping tales
with obscene priests hung over in
the drunkenness of eternal failure.

Paddy O' Sullivan of Kerouac tales
and Cassady visions
Paddy O' Sullivan walking
Washington Square
the bulldozer death lurking everywhere.

Paddy O' Sullivan does your typewriter
still talk to you in
the lonely hours of night?

Paddy O' Sullivan alone in
San Francisco
city of suicides past and present
waiting for that lady poet
who will forgive you in the morning
for forgetting her name in
the hour when our needs are soothed
with the power of the written word
that stirs moves inside us
like a runaway express train stalled
on the freeway
like the haunting breath
of a hound dog closing in for
the kill.

Paddy O' Sullivan where
have all the poets gone walking
straightjackets trapped by time
the sun is not as you see it now
everything changes and yet remains the same
the streets are no more or less intense
the lines on your face are the lines
on my face as we move back into
the body into the inner flesh measured by
the amnesia of yesterday.

this town coughs up its dead most rudely
the raw nerves of time returning to haunt me
oblivious to the thirst lying still at
the edge of the river.

the blueprint of our life etched in
the dark shadows of
the soul.

THE PERFECT ROOM

the murders are carried out with delicate precision
the bodies brought in by hunchbacked sailors
who stay to chat and read from yellow stained
newsprint that they carry like anchors around
their necks leaving at midnight in search
of broken dreams in search of warm thighs braceleted
in snow

on nights like this it is wise not to turn your back
the prophets carry their valuables tied to their
insides and poets can be seen picking
the flowers of the soul leaving their friends
to die in the cold in search of
the perfect poem
the perfect moment seconds before
the hired assassin does them in with lethal
metaphors

still they rise like wounded animals
the muffled cries of death exploding on
the tattooed dawn

Bob Kaufman (Cafe Trieste—1976)

FOR BOB KAUFMAN

Room full of poets, writers, philosophers
drinking the hours away at Spec's bar here
in north beach this cold weekend night
Vicki and the great felony artist waiting
for Fairfax Alix and the midnight party
Patchen's old lady and books translated
into a hundred different tongues.

A table full of beatnik memories
old testament prophets
Micheline and yes you Bob Kaufman
come out of the evening shadows
out from beneath your safe withdrawal
that makes you walk these streets no
longer filled with wonder

sitting at the table reciting yeats
and eliot micheline calls you a titlist
but more than one poets ego is like the
resurrection here at Spec's with the table
running over like the last supper but there
is no rooster to crow your betrayal black
jesus of the fifties

sitting here blinking yesterdays nightmares
a tear came to my eye drinking tonic water
instead of rye calculated madness in the air
no place to dance rainbows buried in the alley
the old god's mixed in with the new

Your long years of silence broken
a prisoner of war come home to tell all
a prisoner of war walking the streets
of north beach
a not so pale ghost come home to tell it all
tell it all eliot and the tea room ball

Your dreams of america are dead
they killed them slower than any war
your dreams of america are deader than
the electricity they shot through your head
in hospital rooms where the blood ran black
not red
But tonight you are alive
thin and trembling like a pale ghost
the protruding veins of your skull
working out their poetic skill
eyes dilated lips trembling
giant come home to taunt
the soldiers
here at Spec's
new but not so new words from the head
soft angel eyes carrying the burden
of past murders on shoulders stooped from
the executioner's sword

POEM FOR THE OLD VANGUARD

they sit talking away
the hours at the bar or at
the triest cafe because it is
the place to go and there is
nothing better to do

they drink and sing their
songs of praise
the silence a gap bridging
the room like
the space between two teeth

pale speed freaks locked
like artists into canvas
tired birds resting on
the shoulders of scarecrows

forgotten prophets crowded into
a dead end street
like a runaway opium pipe in
the hands of a demented
organ grinder

their voices barely audible
going about their daily business
like a gravedigger's shovel scratching
the soft earth in search
of another death.

Gino & Carlo's (Grant and Green)

SATURDAY NIGHT AT GINO AND CARLO'S
—or—
THE MERRY GO ROUND GOES ROUND AND ROUND

I had just finished another campari at
Gino and Carlo's when in walked
Crazy John Yellow Cab's contribution to
The literary scene
And Peter Onstad playing pool next to
The future middleweight champion
Of the world chewing on peanuts shining
Shoes and taking crap from some crusty
Old Italian who wants to lure
Him back to the men's room.

Saturday night at north beach screwed
Up people everywhere wanting to play
With my head bring me back from the dead
Just like farmer john and his wife
The newly weds the dating game
And the Fed's.

One time beauty queen off in the corner
French kissing a longshoreman short on
Sense but long on bread
Well groomed fag standing by
The jukebox playing the part
Of Paul Newman
One eye on the action
The other on the tennis caper kid
Who carries davis cup visions inside
His head.

Sweet Young thing by the telephone booth
Makes with silent groans smiling at
My friend whose name I no longer can recall
Her lips move like a mirror

Her smile Ipana perfect
Real beautiful creature plastic school teacher
Takes down my name for
The liberation front
Shit
I've done it now
I should have stayed in bed
They want me dead
Paranoia
I feel like
J. Edgar Hoover dressed in drag
Dylan is screaming warnings in my ear
Deformed newsboy tugs at my pants leg
He wants to sell me
World War Three

Under any other circumstances
I might join the revolution
But it's damn near
2 a.m.
And i'm going to blow a hell
Of a lot of minds as it is when
I stand up push out my chest
And yell
      S
        H
          A
           Z
          A
            M.

BAD LUCK GAMBLER DIES IN FLAMES

what can you say about
a death like that

the ghost of a nightmare
trapped in all that heat

an insane hotel room with
neon signs and cracked mirrors
for mourners

fate plays strange tricks in
the subconscious of
the minds eye

the image of death calling
her children out to play

like a bad luck gambler
playing out his last
hand

Mooney's Irish Pub

MOONEY'S

30 bored drunks singing
the blues at mooney's
irish pub

a young man lusting for
the cocktail waitress who
beats time to
the grassroots band trying
to drown out
the noise of
the dice players rolling
aces in a low stakes
game

tired dreams shuffling along
the no dance-dance floor
like loose change in
a gambler's pocket

30 bored patrons singing
the blues at mooney's irish
pub on a night
of motionless
motion

MOONEY'S POEM #2

I stumble into Mooney's Irish Pub
somewhere between Grant and Green
in the heart of the old beat
generation

I drink irish coffee and southern
comfort on the rocks backed by
bluegrass music and a blond
cocktail waitress who once rode with
the seventh cavalry

Twenty regular customers at
the bar
no one to get it on with anymore
they don't serve poets at mooney's
not without
the owner's permission

They still do
the irish jig in their imagination
and the bar whiskey is eighty percent proof
all the joys of Saturday night living
condensed into a half dozen carefully
measured drinks

I leave staring at
the stars
my shadow trailing twenty feet behind
another Saturday night drunk
another Sunday morning hangover

SATURDAY MORNING AT THE SUPERMARKET

walking the cold floors of Safeway
food store this winter morning the
air hanging heavy

i eye the angry crowds of shoving
pushing heaving overweight women
loaded down with food and beer and
detergents ready to be carried away
in grocery carts of uncomprehending
terror

my stomach growling ale nightmares
demanding an orange juice and eggs
but no one will let me in front
of them the clerk annoyed at my plight

outside it is raining tired torsos
angels wrap themselves in tinfoil
my ambition to crawl back into bed
remove these clothes and call it
a day

fifteen minutes later outside tasting
the rain finding a ticket on my car
the meter maid disappearing down
the street faster than
my dreams

SATURDAY AFTERNOON AT THE LOCAL LAUNDRYMAT

sitting at the neighborhood laundry
sipping on a pepsi-cola watching
the world tumble around
the dryer

young girl in yellow sweater and
tight blue jeans passes by
on her way to the washer unaware
of the old man bent over
the change machine eying
the middle-aged woman buying
a box of soap powder

it's like watching television
nothing is for real

five more minutes left on
the timer sputtering with
fatigue

five more minutes and it's back in
the laundry bag climb under
the blankets and dream that girl
in yellow is mine

40th BIRTHDAY

i seem to remember wantling writing
a poem about how
he never wanted to be a poet that
he would carry a lunchbox just
like the rest of them if only
the strange mutterings would leave
him alone

now at forty
i feel pretty much the same standing
naked as a deadman's shadow wishing
i had been blessed with
the skills of a union carpenter instead
of these heavy words locked away inside
these aging brain cells

forty years old feeling
like the worn impression on
a buffalo head nickel holding on
to these fading visions
like an immigrant unable to escape
the old country
the moods coming and going
like cloud banks sinking slowly
like the "titanic"
the ghosts dancing on the deck dressed
in words of fire

and as each day brings yet another illusion
harsh as a hobo's dreams
i sing the song of my chosen grave
the lines dancing
like a ballerina on
a high tension wire

while a friend of mine considered
a success in the business world
tells me that like him
i should make a list of priorities
and stick by them no matter what

but the hooks are too far in
too high up into the gut
to do anything about

a poet is like a train
a romantic trip back into another time
he is good for a laugh or two
someone to converse with/occasionally
sleep with/and always someone to stay
away from/when he is down and out

america is no place for
a poet to grow old in
a poet is not a thing
i would want my child to
be.

THE LONE RANGER

drank himself into
a coma before
he was forty
sits around watching
howard cosell eye
alex karras

voted halloween drag queen
of 76   married
tonto's sister and
was murdered in chinatown by
a half breed.

A.D. Winans and Kaye McDonough (Cafe Trieste—Dec., 1976)

THE PARTY GOES ON

Humphrey Bogart is in my dreams
He is framed in stained glass
And Sidney Greenstreet has invaded
My livingroom devouring my food
Joining Jimmy Dean dressed in
Patent leather boots stolen
From Elvis Presley who "revs"
Up his motorcycle while
The keystone cops pound on
My door with napkins for warrants
Stuffing them into my SCM typewriter
Which has been sitting empty for years

Abbot and Costello are killing Texas
Cockroaches with Japanese silkscreen fans
While the vice squad plays monopoly
Refuses to pass go steals
$200 and takes refuge in jail

Shirley Temple is ten years old
Sailing on the Titanic
General Patton trading her toy soldiers
For a quick look up her dress

Groucho Marx pale but growing younger
Smokes cigars with Jack Benny while
Swapping tales of Ponce de Leon
and the fountain of youth

Tonto drops in from the porno flicks
Wrapped in an army blanket stolen
From a confused "linus"
Surrounded by Custer's cavalry
and the Lone Ranger who is courting
Truman Capote's favors

Nixon-Dean-Haldeman and Ford watching
The all night puppet show
Each a pawn in the chess masters' game

Watching the hanging body of Mussolini
Swinging from the chandelier

Cut down the body says
A priest drinking wine from
A goat's flask

Why says Peter Lorre in
A monotonous voice?

Everyone shrugs his shoulders
And the party goes on.

NORTH BEACH WOMAN

    intent italian faces stare
        out at no one in particular
            from the harsh card tables
                at portfino's
the sun shines melted mushrooms
    on the small forgotten shops
        centuries removed from reality
i taste the mid-afternoon glass of wine
    relaxed and alone
        watching the old woman
            with her portly hips
                swinging in the breeze
she carries the looks
    of a hundred lost lovers
        aching with lust
            but the men folk
                do not see her dreaming
                instead
                    of the old country
later the street lights explode
    flashing bombs intruding
        on the ode of time
            but still they go on
                about their business
                    not once bothering to
                look up.

1232 Club

6 A.M. IN NORTH BEACH

6 a.m. in san francisco
the mafia men are beating
on the garbage cans
for those who have not paid
their dues.

rats race across the freeway
like a school of fish playing
mating games.

6 a.m., tomasita halloween
cat whimpers on top of
reeba the earthly dogs back
playing the part of a jockey
in search of the winner's circle
and finding only hunchbacked
sailors from ferlinghetti's dreams
peeking through broken windows
at overheated stallions breathing
hard down the necks of sweating
horses lurking in washington square
where the hangman's shadow stalks
the altar boy counting his heart beat
in dark nightmares of frozen confessionals.

All morning long the night shadows prevail
running up and down the alley scared of
the mad man's dreams being broadcast
on educational t.v. where hope still
glitters like a candle riding
the milky way red with shame searching
the souls of the city demanding
her due crying in dismay at
the mannikin caretakers riding
the sunrise
like a wounded animal kept at bay.

OLD MAN

old man half blind from looking into
the sun too long shuffling along
the wind stroking your hair

forced to look through aching eyes
of one too many summers knowing
life as no one man should staring into
the souls of dead men worshipping
the flowers soon to drape
your coffin

head held low
the dark clouds
of doubt hanging overhead

proud warlock no longer possessed
of magic knocking on sterile doors
destroying all around you shuffling
to the tune of funeral music hiding
in the shadows of streets no longer
filled with wonder

NOTHING COMES CHEAP

they never miss
a first of
the month welfare check
never miss a day at
the bar

they come from cheap
one room hotels eyes
void of rage

not that they didn't
once have it
just that they preferred
evolution to revolution

they carry anger in
their arteries
alcohol in their
blood

haggard faces with forced
smiles who walk
the streets of lost dreams
like a banker without
interest

DEATH WISH

hate stalks the best of men
with flesh weaker than
the heart

the condition of
the poet is no more sacred than
the rooster whose hysterical cries
fill the early morning air when
the elements of innocence
are shed one by one demanding
we compromise with
the darkness that stalks
the soul

some survive transcending
the stars
others use their poems
like a shroud of death
walking from bar to bar
like an undertaker testing
the vein for a last sign
of blood

CITY BLUES

in the back room they sit talking
laughing a poet with a broken
arm nursing a tired grin in
the shadow of an even more tired
afternoon

phantom faces mocking the hours
away in a country that kills
its poets and whose poets kill
each other

a city of sober comedians whose
children resemble w.c. fields
in a city where laughter is
everything and poets a dime
a dozen

Coffee Gallery (Grant and Green)

D.A. LEVY WAS DEAD RIGHT

it's all a lie nothing
changes
the trees shead their leaves
like a summer t.v. special
the undertaker goes about
his business
the walls hide messages
like greedy beggars
the doorbell rings
the telephone rings
nothing changes
it is all the same.

the old man is thinking of death
the young man is thinking of riches
poets have become exotic merchants
of death.

butterflies are beautiful
they have no desire to fly
to the moon
like kaufman says
poets don't sneak into zoos
and talk to tigers anymore
it is perfectly alright
to cast the first stone
if you have more than
the other person

the avon lady walks on water
the blind dog sniffing
his way up her leg.

nothing changes
the boxing matches
the bullfights
the football games go on
and we go on too
like a tired tongue resting
between the legs
of a very bored
woman.

the truth of the matter is that
D.A. Levy was right
               "sum people
just cannot beat the system
               and poets
can't even pretend they are
beating the system."

FOR MILLIE

old millie serving up her flowers
that some say she steals from
the colma graveyard.

old millie singing her songs
like a hotdog vendor at candlestick park
a scratchy victoria record player singing
to tired customers who hang out in
north beach bars
like heavy pennies in a beggar's hand.

old millie carrying her years
like a tired magician with one more
trick up her sleeve.

the terror of the clock counting
down the hours
like a hangman waiting to spring
the trap door.

**UPDATING ALIX'S 185 ANTHOLOGY
OR WHATEVER HAPPENED TO THE
NORTH BEACH POETS AS EXPRESSED
IN THE TITLES OF THEIR POEMS**

bob kaufman still walks
the streets of north beach
explaining to his son parker
the secrets of the ancients and
eugene ruggles commutes from fairfax
singing the beautiful language
remembering women at sea and lines
from an alcoholic ward and sometimes
sleeping in the garden of despair while
waiting for pittsburgh press to make
the proper repairs and
harold norse is holed up on guy street
trying to convince himself that
all poets are in prison and
jack micheline still walks
the streets of north beach clutching
his manuscripts in his hand reminding
us that the world is not for us poor boys and
ruth weiss is still singing of the miracles
that burn in the city that has forgotten
its miracles and
lew welch has disappeared into the backwoods
of despair and
magda is still searching for nobody's whistle and
robert creeley whistles to no one in particular and
kathleen fraser has been court martialed from
the university
her dreams just beyond sight and
jack clifford has left for the mountains speaking
as the wind blows into his body and old dogs dream
whatever it is that old dogs dream while

the sun seeks a new genesis and
frank sears lays cold in his grave and
kaye mc donough writes from union street and
wayne miller chases the shadow of his ancestors
in north beach bars reminding us that there are
no birds alive to sing and
don hutton comes back from the grave to have
thanksgiving dinner at kay coffini's house talking
of needles and the impossible garden and
luke breit has moved to point reyes leaving behind
the blind spot and the books of the dead
for the los angeles refugee poets who
like the mafia have taken over
the trieste cafe and
charles price is making a fortune pirating a cab
losing himself in the structure of his dreams
somewhere beyond the false dawn and
mary stagliano lays cold in the ground and
conyus is looking for geronimo and
ray lopez will always be serving
five years to life and
alix has become a social worker tired
from one too many scars of betrayal and
carl eisinger of junk and my old lady
is trying to find a new way to go and
peter is holed up at the entella drinking
the blood of life from
the undertakers' vein and
bernie has retired his frisbee and
dennis crisp comes and goes undetected
by the legions of the living dead and
Bob Miller is still at gino and carlo's
thinking of the execution days on
the big yard and thinking maybe
i'll take a walk and
george tsongas lives in the dreams

of taurus and
jerome kuleck dreams of nexus and
dean lipton has moved to
the avenues to hide the scars and
stephen levine is publishing
how to books and
shig has left city lights and
city lights has lost its dignity and
jerry kamstra has hired a detective
to find the frisco kid and
janice blue is still singing
janice blue's song and
johnny woodrose is off on his way to boston
searching for the fields of america and
paul kelly is back in prison
a forgotten figure of hungry forests and
rebel mountains.

       2-10-77
       san francisco

GUT RESPONSE TO PETER LE BLANCH'S ART SHOW & ALLEN GINSBERG'S FOR SALE POEM.

Friday Night
November First—1974
Peter Le Blanch
Art Show
De Young Museum
Phillip Whalen in green
Monk Robe
Michael McClure
Harold Norse
David Meltzer presiding
Over a seminar showing
Old slides of city lights
Book store and the trieste cafe
Of north beach days now only
Memories in the ghostly bowels
Of a smiling Buddha

Allen Ginsberg in Lake Tahoe
Tending the property
Lawrence at home tending
The cash register
Wm. Burroughs in a run down
Hotel room
Jack Micheline in
New York City uninvited
Bob Kaufman in north beach
Where it all began getting
Drunk and laughing at
The absurdity of it all

Friday Night
November First—1974
Peter Le Blanch

Art Show
De Young Museum
Phillip Whalen in green
Monk robe
The rest in suits and tie

Allen says in Bastard Angel
That western civilization
Is for sale
Who buys museums
he asks on page twenty-nine?

Who buys art shows
I ask
The sign on the outside says
The National Endowment for
The Arts
That's the government Allen
But then you say me for sale too
On the same page so
I guess you know that we're
All being bought for grants
With some it only takes
A few hundred with others
A few thousand

Ferlinghetti is right on that count
You have to give credit where
Credit is due
You're right Allen
We're all for sale
You're right Allen
    "consciousness for sale
Ego buys all
Ego sells all
Ego for sale
Power for sale."

Friday night
November first—1974
Peter Le Blanch
Art Show.

INSANITY

last years poets writing this years bull-shit
playboy visions haunting the gold coffers
of thousand dollar grants—vegetarian missionaries
hung up on lunatic dreams scratching claws clutching
ammonia images in the arms of naked women shivering
under obscene lightbulbs where crazed moths disappear
inside glass wombs all action carefully recorded
behind steamed windows where eager cheek spread
altar boys eye the electronic marvel coughing
up "johnny carson" commercials every hour on
the hour for overzealous angels of mercy exhibiting
gold lined pussies to impotent doctors reciting
Yeats to pale faced interns hurrying home from
the beauty parlor to masturbating den mothers
eying the results in rooms of leftover orgies
stained with tears where yesterdays poets writing
todays bull-shit dissect the remains of wall street
mad men selling used lobotomy's to the masses
up 13.5 from yesterdays low of -10

City Lights Books (Columbus Avenue)

WINDING DOWN THE HOURS

sitting here in the early morning
hours listening to the sounds of
the city kept company by one lonely
cup of coffee a shot of brandy and
a letter from a girl a thousand
miles away

sitting here winding down the hours
comforted only by a slight breeze
softly caressing the hanging drapes
moving like magic to the sounds of
the hi-fi

my eyes intent following the shadows
on the wall like soft words with
a mood all its own

sitting here watching the night
turn into day the writing desk streaked
with light rays the breeze hiding behind
the curtains the door hungry for someone's
arrival listening to the footsteps of
the morning people preparing for another
day's work the revolving door of reality
opening and closing like a blind man
limping through my dreams

A.D. Winans and Neeli Cherkovski in front of City Lights Publishing House

NEWS FROM NORTH BEACH

they're busy writing my obituary
at north beach as if
i were that important
they're like a pack of doctors
no . . . .
    make that interns . . . .
busy diagnosing my metaphors
dissecting my poems ignoring
the symmetry hidden between
the lines

they have missed their trade
they should have attended
the university majored in
history or archaeology
for they seem quite at home
with the rattling of old bones
unlike their women folk
who are busy unraveling
the mystery of life

the children dancing to
the music their fathers
have never known.

FOR VICKKI

sweet lady
of north beach
body slender as
a picket fence

come crack my skin with
the tenderness
of your tongue

let my fingers be
the warmth between
your legs

you dream of smoke
i'll dream of fire

in the morning
when your defenses
are down

i'll promise
not to hurt
you

BADLAND WOMAN

she's there bringing you
bad memories
like a carnival sideshow freak

she brings you back to
the worse days of your childhood
like a parent intent on making
you pay a long overdue debt

the songs she sings belong
to a forgotten hollywood
matinee idol

she walks your dreams breathing
heavier than an obscene phone caller
carrying her wounds around with her
like a bandage stuck to rotting
flesh.

FOR JILL

walking naked into
the bathroom after
an hour of love making

you tell me that
i'm the best lover
you've ever had

one foot raised to
the sink
like a panama whore

the washcloth wiping away
the seeds
of lust that disappear
faster than
the seconds on
a clock

later
the itch returns
adjusting our bodies to
the height
of acrobatic limits

the flesh trembling
like two tightrope walkers
strung out on
speed

BALL-BUSTER

angry that she married into dullness
and short circuited in
the nightmare of divorce

she rides the heated waters
she rigs to scald me.

her tongue unrolls
like broken string swept under
the carpet of death

the clothes she discards sit
in empty rooms
the passion lost in
the narrow space between
the bed

at night she lays awake
hands crossed with fingernails
that slit the flesh
of bone

she waits for the moon to drain
the energy from your blood
she's at the window bringing rain

her touch as cold as bricks
of ice.

the fractured promises
of her tongue lay hidden
beneath the sun waiting
for revenge which comes when

she is appointed
P.R. man for
God.

FOR CHRISTIE

right away
i can see this chick doesn't
like guys by the way
she warns me that once
she comes
she doesn't like to be touched
and then
she's grabbing my head and telling
me to do it soft and nice like and
don't bite and the clit is sensitive
like i'm somehow new to this
sort of thing and then
she's squeezing my head and
making those familiar sounds and when
she comes she pushed me off lights
up a cigarette and tells me
it's time to go

baby
you don't have to have balls
to be a chauvinist pig

UNTITLED

this empty rooms whispers
dead secrets
old ghosts disappear
reappear to shake
my hand.

the telephone is
the only one
with connections according
to my agent ––
who returns my manuscripts
postage due ––
and you insist on standing in
the kitchen butcher knife
in hand looking
the part of a mad doctor
hacking the limbs off
a dead tree.

the cat stalks
the porch with
ruby eyes
the dog bored with
the whole show.

in the corner on
the mantle
my father's old photograph
looks back at me
with accusing eyes.

death lurks everywhere
licking every crevice
of the room.

she will find what
she seeks
my grandmother warned
me of this.

death
the noble savage
death
the avenging sadist
leaving behind
the scars playing
out the game to
the bitter end.

a giant hearse among
a sea of compact
cars.

NORTH BEACH POEM

out into
the harsh night into
the lonely streets
of north beach stoned
on words walking
the streets of san francisco watching
the old people make their way to mass

old men and women leaving behind their sins
dressed in simple hats and death black shawls
bowing to the holy eternal mumble
of dead saints dressed in gold thirsting
for the wine that is denied them

the ceiling a giant mirror hidden in
the skulls of expressionless monks laying
in glass coffins
hands folded in ecstasy
eyes open smiling like a stoned gypsy
hanging from a pendulum in
the chapel of hope where italian priests
weaned on dago red ply evil thoughts from
sterile minds toying with
the heads of the masses staring always
staring searching for paradise
fat and content smoking tiajuana slims
stone faced magicians on their way to
the graveyard where semen ejaculating
altar boys mock the hunchback crawling
on scarred knees three steps behind
the screaming organ grinder with
the one-eyed monkey on his back

san francisco
home of my birth where
iowa scarecrows peek through broken

windows at overheated stallions breathing
hard down the necks of sweating dwarfs lurking in
the back yard of grace cathedral where
the hangman's shadow stalks
the altar boy with neon signs of insecurity

no dogs allowed
no parking between nine and five
keep off the grass
do not enter
out of order
one way
do not disturb

ford smiling
kissinger smiling
justice bound and gagged in chicago

youth cult found inside pants pocket
of man claiming to be
ponce de leon

walking the night
walt whitman in search
of sherwood anderson lost
in clown alley sniffing used
ashtrays

whore screws
cocksuckers delight
ten dollars a night
hank williams twenty years
ahead of his time

robin hood strung out on speed
breastless majorette with greased
thighs caresses phallic baton stuck
between plastic legs

fat ass politicians selling
their version of freedom
bent over with the weight
of their medals

up, up and away

superman is alive and well
at gino and carlo's disguised
as a dissipated italian gone
mad on kryptonite

here on grant and green where
the black and white hustle nightly
a cargo of restless souls for
city prisons late midnight
special

chinatown lamps
oriental intrigue
do chinese women really
have slanted cunts?

the tong won't ell you
they're too damn busy
selling lottery tickets
down in shanty town

the left
the right
the overground
the underground
all busy ripping off
the other while
the penis fantasy
of a vaginal orgasm finds
clitoral satisfaction in
the extracted womb

of the madonna hung
out on the clothesline
to dry

2 a.m.
young men standing half out
of their heads
young girls in jeans and
see-through minds

old men not all that old stare
vacantly at the moon at
the women who carry their souls
in their eyes

walking past central police station recalling
the holding cell where young "ed"
i never knew his last name picked
at his head cracked open by
a barker in a broadway tunnel
of love

walking to crazy john's place sharing
a glass of wine sharing even
the paranoia chatting with
frank at the bus stop on
my way back to mission street
his eyes as large as
the owl who haunts
my dreams

you can find them all here
on any given night
an all night orgy
no invite needed

crazy eugene who crushed
the skulls of those who
disagreed with him but
who went to oregon and
found himself in
the eyes of his children

peter with dreams
of picasso who walks
the open artery
of a dying wound

lorraine stoned on
coke and meth
alix back from petaluma
to recite
mc beth

here in north beach where
they took eddie away and
gave him three years and
eyes that weep blood then
set him free again
one thousand-ninety-five
days and nights
of cell and sodomy with
only a handful
of angry poems that
no longer crack
the looking glass

here in north beach where
they come and go suffocating on
the water of sound

home of paddy o' sullivan
forgotten legend
of his time

home of bob kaufman giant
of a north beach that
no longer exists

home of jerome whose visions
of nexus faded in
mendocino state hospital where
you can't always tell
the difference between
a smile and a scream

home of ben although
no more who after ninety
days treatment
they drove thoroughly mad
no doubt for his own good
when they traded him straight up
his heritage for
a feather bed

but it need not be here
it can happen anywhere
like they ran in
jack micheline for
pissing on a cop's foot
in new york city
for biting a law man's nose
but they couldn't kill
the poetry and prose and
now he's back twice as dangerous
as before

and they messed with bukowski's face
for offering them salvation and grace
not understanding anything but guns and mace

but they can't take away the soul of vickki
of pale thighs and eyes that know no lies

vickki whose good times i have shared and
whose pain i have known
nor the spirit of the woman of one-eight-five
whose deeds are legendary

and yet they took away inez
who few if any of you recall

inez of fine breasts and limbs
of fire who died alone in
a beatnik san gottardo hotel hall

they took away d.a. levy's life pulled
the trigger as sure as his own because
he was human enough to believe
he could change this land

and they took the life
of ed lipman but could not break
his spirit for
he knew the secret of invisibility something
the hound dogs can only smell

from broadway to mission street where
the pigs are a different breed junkies
sitting at the doggie diner needles
in search of sunken veins making their
own dreams their own buddha their own
jesus christ

to them city prison is just another room
where the roaches crawl sideways up
the wall on their way to
a beggar's coffin where
the bones are many

working my way home from north beach
to upper mission passing
kell's place where
the lonely man of music lies arms
tight around his woman's head
to keep the clouds of death away
so that at least she might sleep

home at last
safe from the self-appointed gods
of my destiny tired
of what they want for you and
me when it is really them

tired that they will follow me to
the grave their sons of death bringing
more death to mine

at a time like this
it is good to be alone
no one to camouflage your feelings
bandage my dreams

hung up on my own disappointments
like an animal playing solitaire
with his shadow

the hi-fi playing low and kind deadening
the screams of my mind oblivious to
the outside ferris wheel revolving around
the universe housing fragile bodies moving
like silent boxcars across angry railroad tracks
where lonely souls drag themselves along
the freeway scrambling like wounded animals wrapped
in fear and angry poets spit out funeral wreathes
at scarred clouds passing slowly across
the face of the moon

ABOUT THE AUTHOR

A.D. Winans was born in San Francisco, and resided in the North Beach area for many years before moving to the Mission district where he now lives. A graduate of San Francisco State University; his work has appeared in over 200 literary journals and anthologies. He is the author of *Carmel Clowns* (Atom Mind Publications), *Crazy John Poems* (Grande Ronde Press), *Tales of Crazy John* (Second Coming Press), *Straws of Sanity* (Thorp Springs Press), and *Venus in Pisces* (Golden Mt. Press).